D1408550

BLAST

School Outreach

Carnegie Library of Pittsburgh

DEMCO

Family Center
LIBRARY CENTER

OCTOBER
PATTERNS, PROJECTS & PLANS

by
Imogene Forte

Family Center
LIBRARY CENTER

Incentive Publications, Inc.
Nashville, Tennessee

CARNEGIE LIBRARY OF PITTSBURGH

Illustrated by Gayle Seaberg Harvey
Cover by Susan Eaddy
Edited by Sally Sharpe

ISBN 0-86530-126-3

Copyright © 1989 by Incentive Publications, Inc., Nashville, Tennessee. All rights reserved. Permission is hereby granted to the purchaser of one copy of OCTOBER PATTERNS PROJECTS & PLANS to reproduce, in sufficient quantities to meet yearly classroom needs, pages bearing the following statement:

© 1989 by Incentive Publications, Inc., Nashville, TN.

Table of Contents

PREFACE

October — a many-splendored month

OCTOBER . . .

. . . A TIME of color majesty — red and gold, green and brown, pumpkin orange, purple and blue, midnight black and moonglow yellow.

. . . A TIME of visions of delight, inside and outside — morning dew, midday shimmer, sunsets of every hue, and magical and mysterious nighttime skies.

. . . A TIME of scents and scenes to sense and savor — simmering spices, popcorn popping and cookies baking, apples on trees and cider in mugs, licorice sticks, candle glow and pumpkins' faces, falling leaves, thistle heads and crimson berries, nuts and squirrels, football games, scarecrows in the fields and goldenrod along city sidewalks.

. . . A TIME of seasonal excitement — black cats, spiders and bats, jolly jack-o'-lanterns, masks and costumes, parties and tricks and treats.

All of this and more is the magic of October waiting to be brought right into your "come alive" classroom. Watch students' smiles widen and their eyes brighten as the magic of October greets them from the ceiling to the floor, from windows and doors, from work sheets and activity projects, from stories and books, and especially from an enthusiastic, "project planned" teacher.

This little book of OCTOBER PATTERNS, PROJECTS & PLANS has been put together with tender loving care to help you be prepared to meet every one of the school days in October with special treats, learning projects and fun surprises that will make your students eager to participate in every phase of the daily schedule and look forward to the next day. Best of all, the patterns, projects and plans are ready for quick and easy use and require no elaborate materials and very little advance preparation.

For your convenience, the materials in this book have been organized around four major unit themes. Each of the patterns, projects and plans can be used independently of the unit plan, however, to be just as effective in classrooms in which teachers choose not to use a unit approach. All are planned to complement and enrich adopted curriculum schemes and to meet young children's interests and learning needs.

Major unit themes include:
- October's Here!
- Fables, Fairy Tales and Nursery Rhymes
- Fire Prevention Week
- Halloween

Each unit includes a major objective and things to do; poster/booklet cover, bulletin board or display; patterns; art and/or an assembly project; reproducible basic skills activities; and book, story and poem suggestions to make the literature connection.

Other topics, special days and events for which patterns, projects and plans have been provided include:

- Autumn's Natural Treasures
- Columbus Day (Second Monday in October)
- Noah Webster's Birthday (October 16)
- The Nighttime Sky
- National Popcorn Week (Last Week in October)
- Dinosaurs

OCTOBER'S HERE!

Major Objective:
Children will develop awareness of the colors, sights, sounds, seasonal changes, and events that characterize the month of October.

Things To Do:

- Children will have fun making and wearing October headbands on the first October school day (page 18)! This builds group identity and class pride as well as seasonal awareness.

- Let the children use strips of red, green and brown crepe paper to "dance" the *Autumn Leaf* poem on page 19!

- Give each child a tree pattern (page 21) and ask the child to cut out one red, yellow or brown leaf to paste on the tree. Have the children tell stories about "the last leaf on the tree."

- To make the literature connection, read *Word Bird's Fall Words*, *The Oxford Picture Word Book*, *Seasons*, *Pumpkin, Pumpkin*, and *Heckedy Peg* (see pages 77 & 78).

- Help the children use the patterns in this book to make decorations for doors, windows, desks and bookcases. Use the mini-patterns to add pizazz to work sheets and messages!

- Send the "letter to parents" (page 10) home to annouce the month's plans and to ask for donations for your materials collection. Check your supplies to be sure you are ready for the month!

To complete the activities in this book, you will need:

- construction paper (assorted colors)
- crepe paper (orange, red, green, brown)
- white tissue paper & facial tissues
- flannel (for flannel board activity)
- paper clips
- rubber bands
- tape (cellophane & masking)
- twigs or craft sticks
- paste
- tempera paint (black, orange, green, red, brown, yellow)
- typing paper

- paintbrushes
- scissors
- pencils
- crayons & markers
- stapler
- paper plates, cups & napkins
- yarn, ribbon, buttons, pipe cleaners & other misc. materials
- small, medium & large paper bags
- newspaper
- drinking straws
- popcorn (lollipops & candy, optional)

Dear Parents,

October's here! In our classroom, that means that it is a time of good cheer and color majesty; a time of visions of delight, inside and outside; a time of scents and scenes to sense and savor; and a time of seasonal excitement — black cats, spiders and bats, jolly jack-o'-lanterns, masks and costumes, parties, and tricks and treats.

All of this and more is the magic of October at school. We will read, write, dance, sing and act out stories, books, poems and songs; add, subtract, and count; cut, paste, draw, paint and assemble art projects; experiment and explore; and continue to learn, live, and work together.

During the month your child will bring home art projects; math, science, and language activities; and stories, songs and games to share with you. Please take the time to stop, look, listen, question and enjoy these special projects. Your participation is a very important part of the whole learning experience.

In order to help with our projects, you can collect empty shoe boxes; clean coffee, shortening, or potato chip cans; egg cartons; and orange, red, green, gold and brown yarn, ribbon and tissue paper. You also can share with us favorite fairy tales, nursery rhymes, fables and stories that you think we might miss. You might even like to come to class to tell or read some of these to the children. We would like that.

Sincerely,

© 1989 by Incentive Publications, Inc., Nashville, TN.

OCTOBER ALPHABET

A . . . Apple butter, apple cider and apple pie

B . . . Bats, black cats and busy boys

C . . . Christopher Columbus who sailed the ocean blue

D . . . Days of autumn splendor

E . . . Everywhere, everywhere, October's colors are to be seen

F . . . First frosts on the windowpane

G . . . Ghosts, goblins and gremlins

H . . . Halloween, of course!

I . . . Ichabod Crain who was chased by the headless horseman

J . . . Jack-o'-lanterns, fat and squat or lean and mean

K . . . Knowing all about October's wonders

L . . . Leaves tumbling down, leaves on the ground

M . . . Monsters — marvelous and mean, all dressed up for Halloween

N . . . Nighttime skies

O . . . Owls in trees

P . . . Pumpkins piled high in the patch

Q . . . Quail, a bird to be spotted in October fields

R . . . Red and gold, green and brown, autumn colors all around

S . . . Scary scarecrows

T . . . Treats instead of tricks

U . . . Ugly witches, toads and bats

V . . . Vegetables to gather from October gardens

W . . . Witches on the prowl

X . . . XXX's for October kisses

Y . . . Yellow flowers along the roadside

Z . . . Zombies, that boys and girls may pretend to be on Halloween

© 1989 by Incentive Publications, Inc., Nashville, TN.

OCTOBER

SUNDAY	MONDAY	TUESDAY	WEDNESDAY	THURSDAY	FRIDAY	SATURDAY

© 1989 by Incentive Publications, Inc., Nashville, TN.

HOW TO USE
THE OCTOBER CALENDAR

Use the calendar to:

. . . find on what day of the week the first day of October falls.

. . . count the number of days in October.

. . . find the number on the calendar which represents October.

. . . mark the birthdays of "October babies" in your room.

. . . mark special days

- Child Health Day (October 3)
- National School Lunch Week (Second Week in October)
- Columbus Day (Second Monday in October)
- World Food Day (October 16)
- Noah Webster's Birthday (October 16)
- Halloween (October 31)
- National Popcorn Week (Last week in October)
- etc.

CALENDAR ART

© 1989 by Incentive Publications, Inc., Nashville, TN.

OCTOBER CLASSROOM MANAGEMENT CHART

© 1989 by Incentive Publications, Inc., Nashville, TN.

CLASSROOM HELPERS

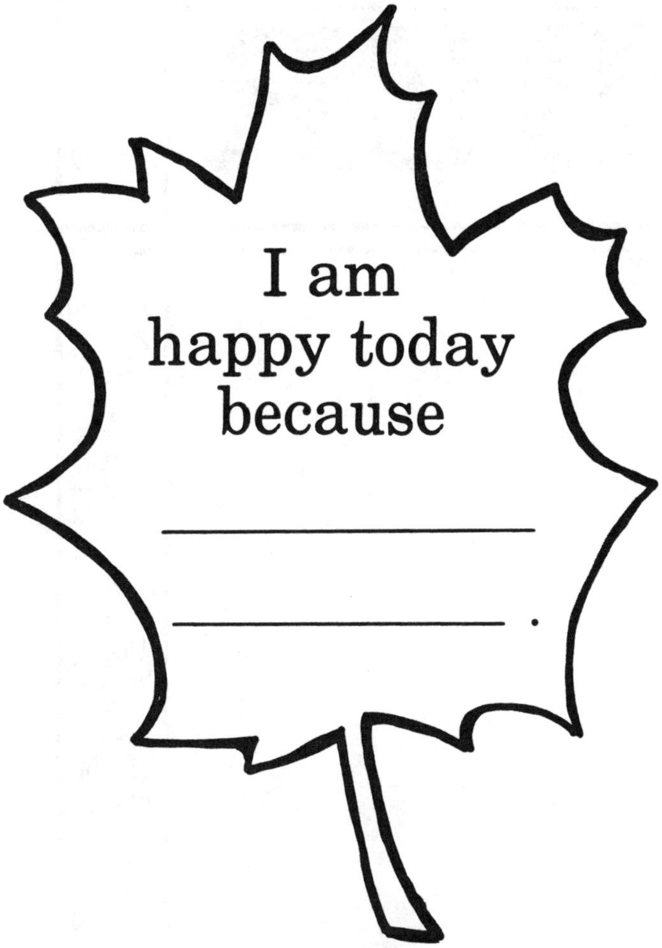

I am
happy today
because

_____

_____ .

Teacher's
Helper

Friendship Award

To: _____

For: _____

_____ Teacher

_____ Date

Top Pumpkin Award

To: _____

For: _____

© 1989 by Incentive Publications, Inc., Nashville, TN.

OCTOBER

© 1989 by Incentive Publications, Inc., Nashville, TN.

OCTOBER DOORKNOB DECORATION

Color and cut out this doorknob decoration.
Hang it on your door to tell the world that you are happy about
October's golden days.

IT'S TIME TO CHEER — OCTOBER IS HERE!

© 1989 by Incentive Publications, Inc., Nashville, TN.

Cut out the October headband and paste it on a strip of construction paper sized to fit the child's head. Fasten the headband with a paper clip.

© 1989 by Incentive Publications, Inc., Nashville, TN.

AUTUMN LEAVES ARE FALLING

Autumn leaves
   Falling, falling,
Autumn leaves are
   Falling down.

Red and green,
   Gold and brown,
Autumn leaves
   On the ground.

Autumn leaves
   Red and green,
Gold and brown,
   Falling all around.

Autumn leaves
   Falling, falling,
Autumn leaves are
   Falling down.

© 1989 by Incentive Publications, Inc., Nashville, TN.

Construction:
1. Reproduce the tree pattern (page 21) and color it with markers or cut it out of construction paper.
2. Use the patterns on page 22 to cut autumn leaves out of construction paper. Write a special treat for the day on each leaf.
   Examples: Today the class will enjoy ten extra minutes of recess.
   We will have a popcorn snack this afternoon.
3. Cut the caption "October's Treasures" out of construction paper and assemble the board as shown above. (Attach the leaves to the tree with the "blank" sides showing.)
4. Each day, turn over a leaf and let the children enjoy a special treat!

© 1989 by Incentive Publications, Inc., Nashville, TN.

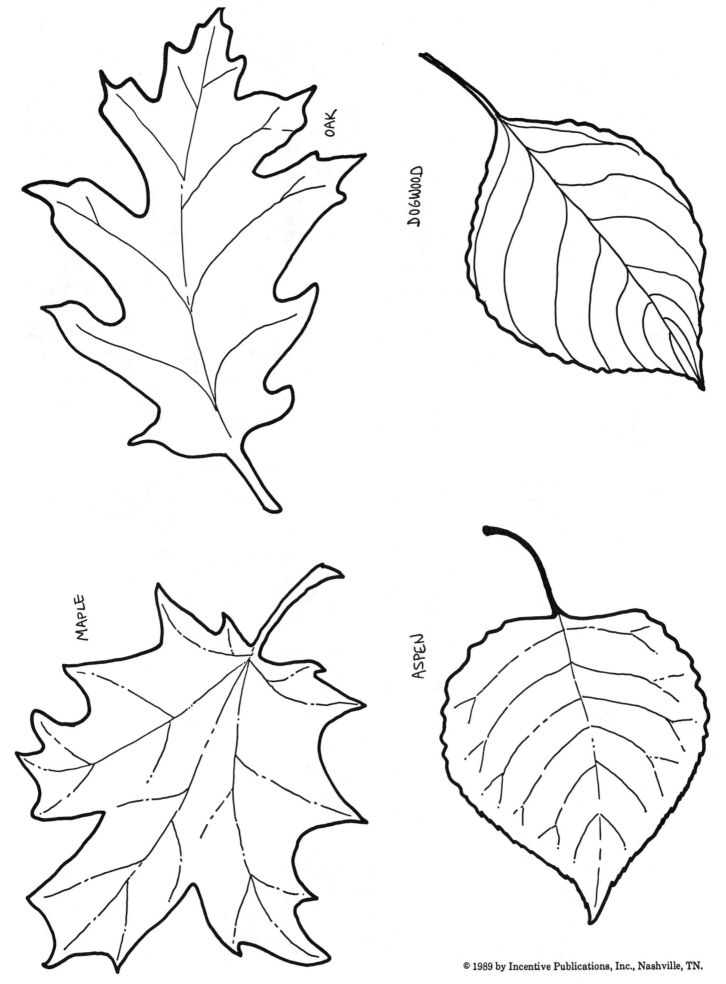

OAK

DOGWOOD

MAPLE

ASPEN

© 1989 by Incentive Publications, Inc., Nashville, TN.

© 1989 by Incentive Publications, Inc., Nashville, TN.

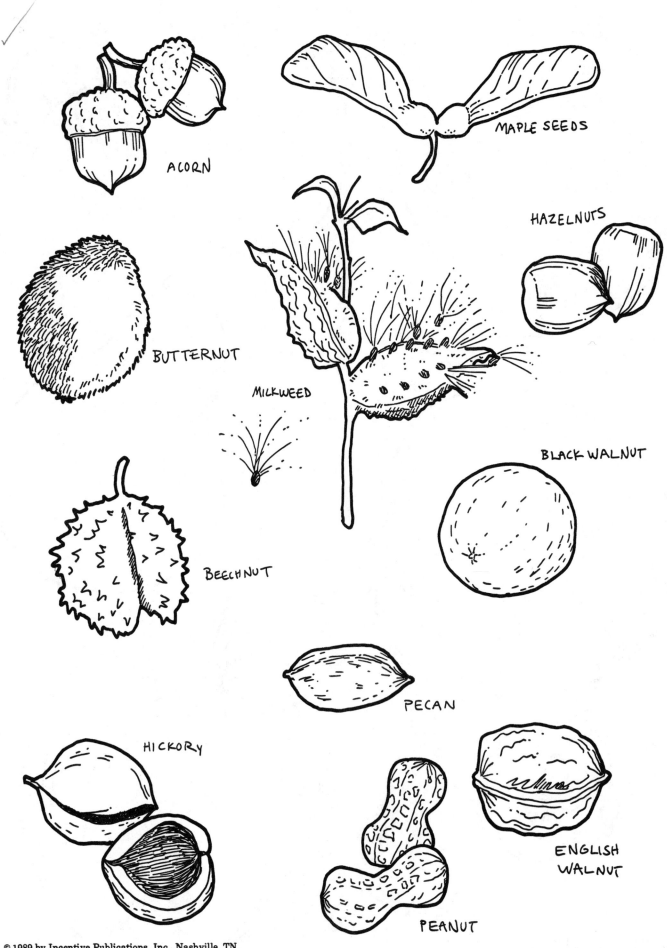

ACORN

MAPLE SEEDS

HAZELNUTS

BUTTERNUT

MILKWEED

BLACK WALNUT

BEECHNUT

PECAN

HICKORY

ENGLISH WALNUT

PEANUT

© 1989 by Incentive Publications, Inc., Nashville, TN.

© 1989 by Incentive Publications, Inc., Nashville, TN.

© 1989 by Incentive Publications, Inc., Nashville, TN.

— GOLDENROD —

— MUMS —

BLACK-EYED SUSANS —

— MARIGOLDS —

©1989 by Incentive Publications, Inc., Nashville, TN.

Construction:

1. Reproduce the ship pattern (page 29) and color it with markers or cut it out of construction paper.
2. Write the caption "Columbus Sailed The Ocean Blue In Fourteen Hundred And Ninety-Two" on a construction paper banner.
3. Cut ocean "waves" out of blue construction paper or butcher paper.
4. Assemble the board as shown above.

Variation:

- Add two ships and substitute the caption "Three Ships Set Sail For A New Land." Help the children learn the names of the ships. Tell or read a story about the voyage.

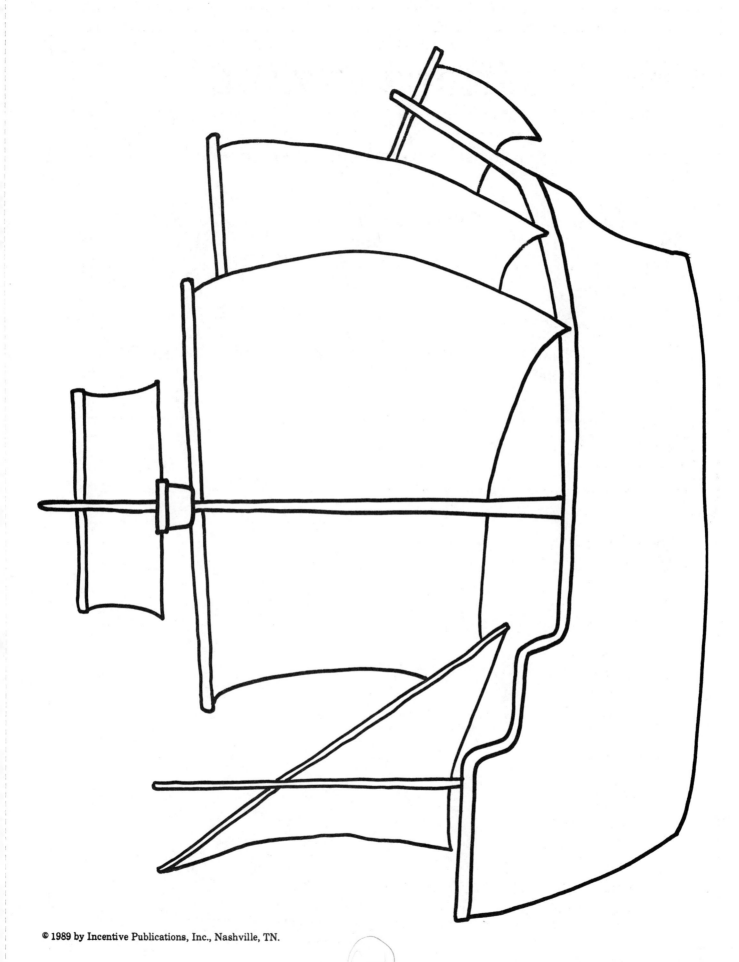

© 1989 by Incentive Publications, Inc., Nashville, TN.

A FAMOUS VOYAGE

Here's a little rhyme to help you remember when Columbus sailed to America.

Columbus sailed the ocean blue
In fourteen hundred and ninety-two

Draw a picture of something we have today that Columbus would be surprised to see.

Name _____

SILLY SHIPS

Circle the silly mistake on each ship.
Color everything except the mistakes.

Finding mistakes
© 1989 by Incentive Publications, Inc., Nashville, TN.

OCTOBER WORDS

Noah Webster was the author of the first English dictionary.
He was born on October 16, 1758.
To celebrate his birthday, add your own October words and pictures to
the list below.

leaf

pumpkin

ghost

scarecrow

squirrel

pear

bat

FABLES, FAIRY TALES AND NURSERY RHYMES

Major Objective:
Children will develop appreciation of fables, fairy tales and nursery rhymes; will be able to identify with fictional characters, settings and events; and will become aware of simple plot and sequence development.

Things To Do:

- Create an October bulletin board (page 34) that can be modified for Children's Book Week (November 13 - 19). Use the board as a showcase for fables, fairy tales and nursery rhymes featuring scarecrows, crows, pumpkins and nighttime skies.

- Reproduce the nighttime skies nursery rhymes (page 39) for each child and read the rhymes to the children. Instruct the children to ask family members to observe the nighttime sky with them. Discuss what the children have observed.

- Sing or chant *Twinkle, Twinkle, Little Star.* Have each child name one thing he or she would wish for and tell how his or her life would be changed if the wish were granted. Read *The Three Wishes* to make the literature connection (see page 78).

- Have the children use yellow and orange crayons to draw nighttime sky pictures. Prepare a thin black tempera wash to paint over the pictures.

- Use the crow, fox and tree patterns (pages 21 & 38) to make flannel board figures to be used in telling the fable of the fox and the crow. Ask the children to tell what the "message" of the fable is.

- Use the star pattern (page 37) to make reading awards.

- Reproduce the pumpkin pattern (page 40) for each child:

  Read *Peter, Peter Pumpkin Eater* (see *Mother Goose*, page 77). Ask each child to draw a picture of what he or she would keep inside the pumpkin shell.

  Read *Cinderella* (see *A Fairy Tale Treasury*, page 77). Ask the children to add features to turn the pumpkin into a coach for Cinderella.

GOOD BOOKS ARE WORTH CROWING ABOUT!

Construction:
1. Reproduce the scarecrow, full moon, and crow patterns (pages 36-38) and color them with markers or cut them out of construction paper.
2. Cut the caption "Good Books Are Worth Crowing About!" out of construction paper.
3. Assemble the board as shown above.
4. Display the children's book reports or illustrations of favorite books on the board.

Variation:
- Cut additional crows out of black construction paper to perch atop the children's work.

Construction:

1. Reproduce the scarecrow, half moon and pumpkin patterns (pages 36, 37 & 40) and color them with markers or cut them out of construction paper.
2. Cut the caption "We're Not Scared Of Hard Work!" out of construction paper.
3. Assemble the board as shown above.
4. Display the children's work on the pumpkins.

© 1989 by Incentive Publications, Inc., Nashville, TN.

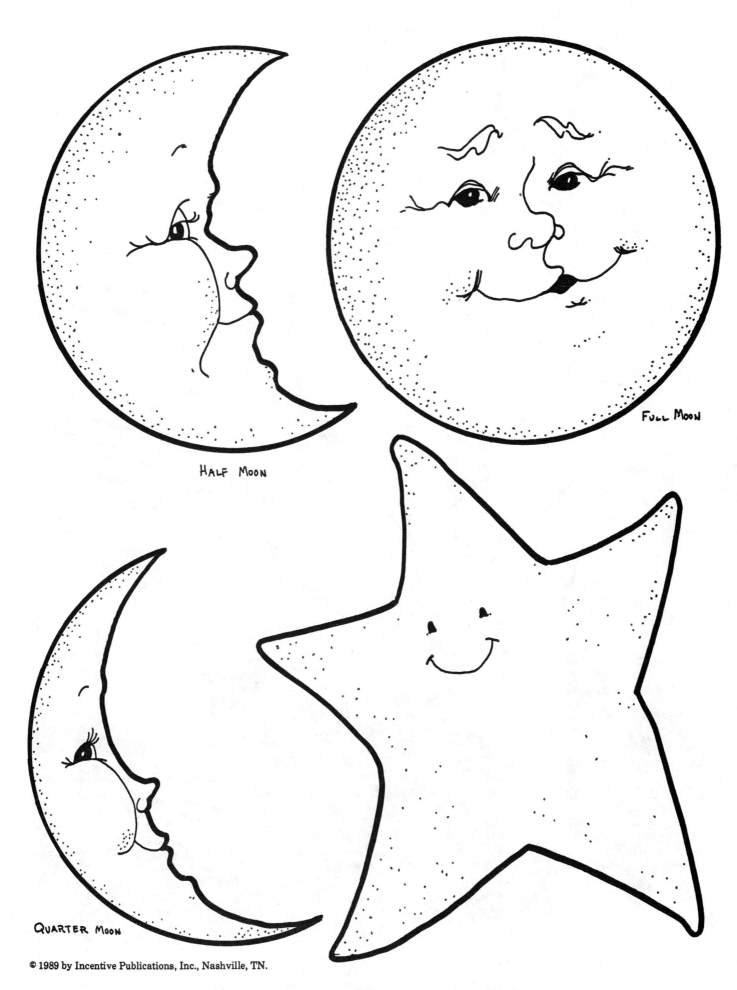

HALF MOON

FULL MOON

QUARTER MOON

© 1989 by Incentive Publications, Inc., Nashville, TN.

© 1989 by Incentive Publications, Inc., Nashville, TN.

NIGHTTIME SKIES

Twinkle, Twinkle Little Star

Twinkle, twinkle little star,
How I wonder what you are.

Up above the world so high,
Like a diamond in the sky.

Twinkle, twinkle little star,
How I wonder what you are.

A Moon Song

Who hung his hat on the moon?
The owl in his bubble balloon.
One bright summer night
He sailed out of sight,
And, hooting like Lucifer,
*   hung in delight*
His three-cornered hat on the moon.

Star Light, Star Bright

Star light,
Star bright,
First star I see tonight . . .
I wish I may
I wish I might
Have the wish
I wish tonight.

Hey, Diddle Diddle

Hey, diddle diddle
The cat and the fiddle,
The cow jumped over the moon.
The little dog laughed to see
*   such sport,*
And the dish ran away with the
*   spoon.*

The Man In The Moon

The man in the moon came down too soon
*   To inquire the way to Norridge;*
The man in the south, he burnt his mouth
*   With eating cold plum porridge.*

© 1989 by Incentive Publications, Inc., Nashville, TN.

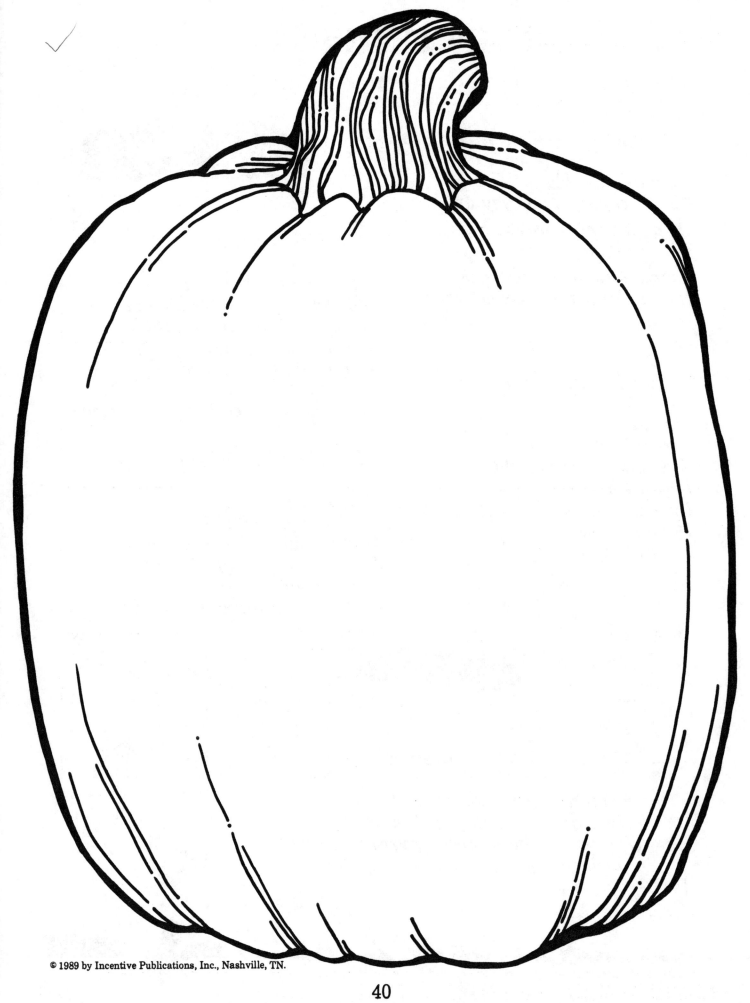

© 1989 by Incentive Publications, Inc., Nashville, TN.

COUNT THE PUMPKINS

Cut and paste the numerals in the correct boxes.
How many pumpkins are there on this page? _____

CINDERELLA FINGER PUPPETS

Color and cut out the puppets.
Tape the puppets together.
Act out the story.

© 1989 by Incentive Publications, Inc., Nashville, TN.

FIRE PREVENTION WEEK

Major Objective:
Children will develop knowledge about and appreciation for National Fire Prevention Week, will become familiar with the people and equipment associated with fire safety, and will practice safety precautions and procedures.

Things To Do:

- Tell the children that National Fire Prevention Week is the second week in October. This is because on October 8, 1871, Mrs. O'Leary's cow kicked over a lighted lantern which started the great Chicago fire. The fire left nearly 100,000 people homeless. Ask these questions: What would happen if this many people were homeless in your town? How long do you think it took to rebuild the homes? What do you think happened to Mrs. O'Leary's cow?

- Reproduce, distribute and discuss the fire drill safety rules (page 44). Have the children illustrate fire drill safety in the space provided. Stage a practice fire drill so that the children may learn what to do when the fire signal is sounded.

- Let the children use toy telephones to role play calling the fire department to report a fire. Teach the children the emergency numbers for your area. Use the homework wrist band (page 46) for reinforcement.

- Let one day be "fire safety day." Discuss fire safety rules, have the children use the patterns on pages 45 and 46 to make fire safety posters, and present "fire safety specialist" badges (page 46).

- Demonstrate the use of a fire extinguisher and discuss how it works.

- Discuss the firefighter's job as well as the jobs of other community helpers. Plan a field trip to a fire station, or invite a firefighter to visit the class.

- Sing and act out the song *I'm A Big Red Fire Truck* (page 47). Let the children make up other verses!

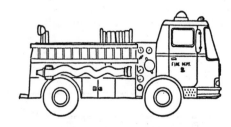

FIRE DRILL
SAFETY RULES

1. When the fire bell rings, stop what you are doing and listen to the teacher.
2. Line up and follow the leader outside the building.
3. Stay with your group.
4. Stand still and be very quiet until you are told what to do next.

Draw a picture to show fire drill safety.

© 1989 by Incentive Publications, Inc., Nashville, TN.

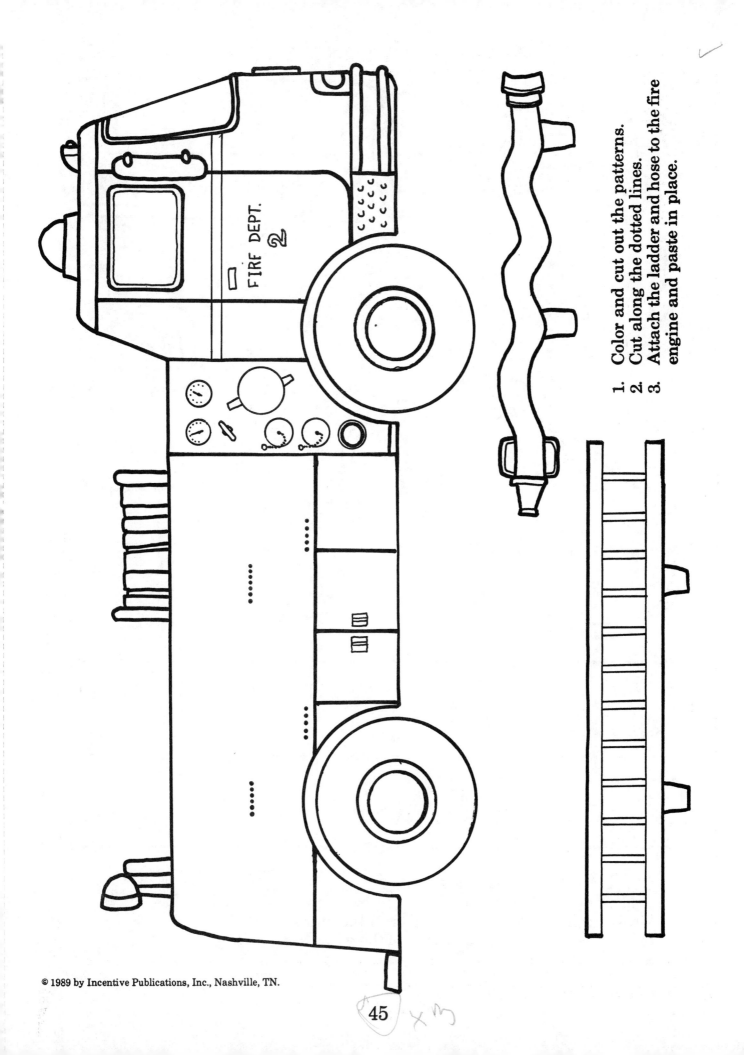

1. Color and cut out the patterns.
2. Cut along the dotted lines.
3. Attach the ladder and hose to the fire engine and paste in place.

FIRE DEPT. 2

© 1989 by Incentive Publications, Inc., Nashville, TN.

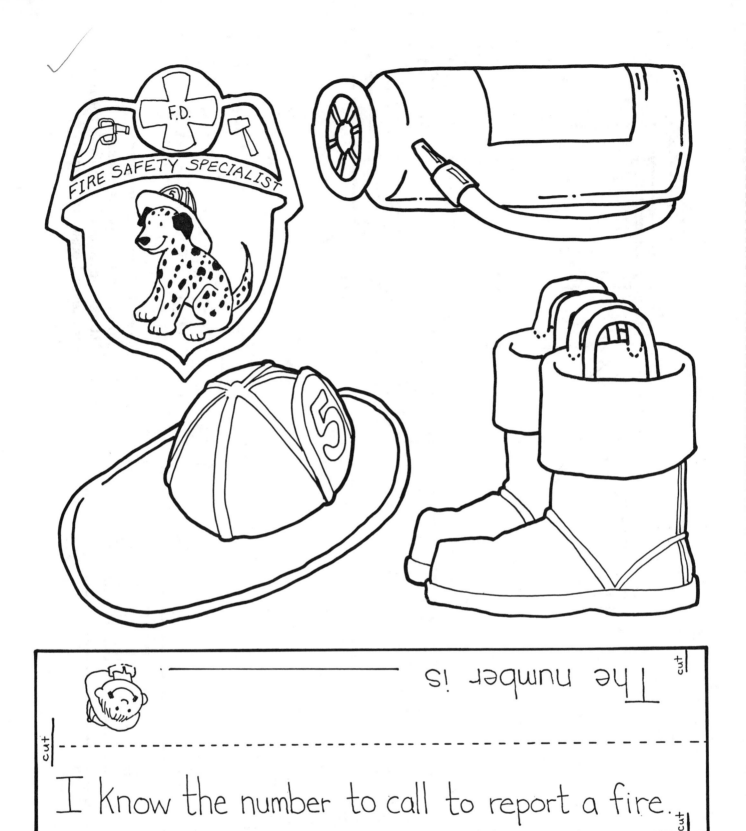

The number is _____

I know the number to call to report a fire.

1. Cut out the homework wrist band.
2. Fold along the dotted lines.
3. Write the correct telephone number in the blank.
4. Cut where indicated and assemble the wrist band around the child's arm.

© 1989 by Incentive Publications, Inc., Nashville, TN.

I'M A BIG RED FIRE TRUCK

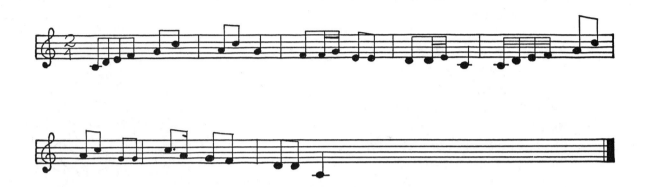

Sung to the tune of *I'm A Little Teapot.*

I'm a big red fire truck long and stout,
When I am needed I roar and shout,
People love to see me rush about,
Just turn me on and head me out.

I'm a big red fire truck stout and long,
Here is my ladder, tall & strong,
When I get a call you'll hear my song,
Just climb aboard and turn me on.

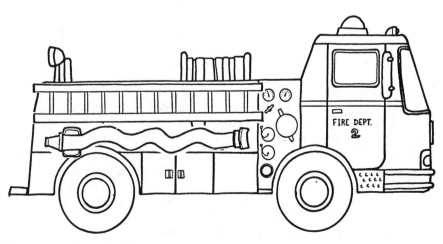

© 1989 by Incentive Publications, Inc., Nashville, TN.

SOMETHING'S POPPING

Celebrate National Popcorn Week (last week in October) with a party, picnic, parade, popper-stopper personalities, popover, poetry, or a pop-up play. Whichever you choose, you will need to begin with a big bowl of popping good popcorn!

- First, read this poem to the group and then use it as an easy "act out" choral reading.

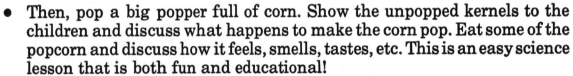

> *Plinkety-plink, plink*
> *Drop the kernels in the pot*
> *Sizzle-zzz-zzz*
> *Let the oil get good and hot*
> *Shake—rustle—rustle*
> *Move each restless little fellow*
> *'til he bursts full grown*
> *A fluffy white or yellow*
> *Sprinkle—lightly—lightly*
> *To season — oh, so nice*
> *Crunch—munch—munch*
> *Serve with soda pop and ice!*

- Then, pop a big popper full of corn. Show the unpopped kernels to the children and discuss what happens to make the corn pop. Eat some of the popcorn and discuss how it feels, smells, tastes, etc. This is an easy science lesson that is both fun and educational!
- Save some of the popcorn for . . .

Old Fashioned Popcorn Balls

What to use:

large saucepan & wooden spoon
hot plate or stove
15 c popped popcorn
1 c corn syrup
1/2 c water
1 tbs. butter
extra butter for greasing your hands!

large bowl
measuring cups and spoons
wax paper
1 c molasses
1/2 c sugar
1/2 tsp. salt
1 tbs. vanilla

What to do:

1. Place popcorn in large container and spread wax paper over work area.
2. Place molasses, corn syrup, sugar and water in saucepan to boil. Boil until a little of the mixture forms a hard ball when put in water.
3. Remove the pan from heat and stir in salt, butter and vanilla. Cool for 3 minutes.
4. Butter your hands. Slowly pour the syrup over the popcorn and stir with your hands.
5. Mold the caramelized corn into any kind of shape. Place on wax paper to dry.

© 1989 by Incentive Publications, Inc., Nashville, TN.

These make great Halloween party treats, too!

POPCORN
SCULPTURES

Use drinking straws, pipe cleaners, yarn, paper clips, buttons and bows, a little paste, and a lot of creativity to make popcorn sculptures.

These shapes also can be used as clip art for bulletin boards, work sheets, messages, etc The turtle can be used as a pin-on award!

© 1989 by Incentive Publications, Inc., Nashville, TN.

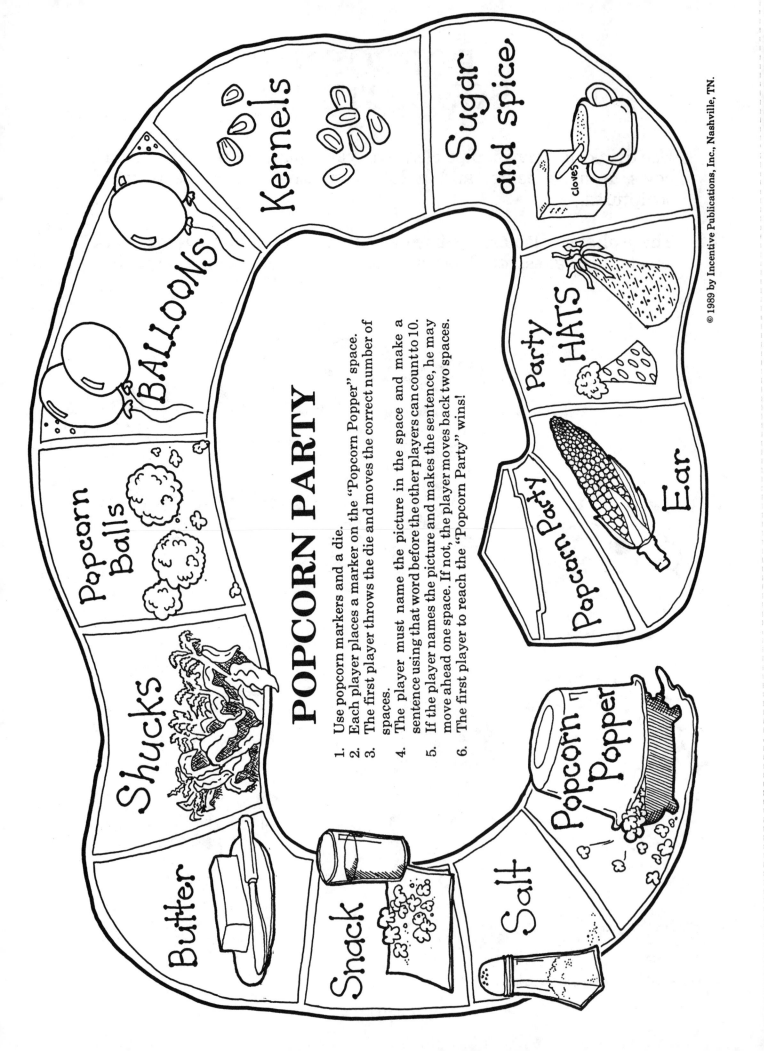

POPCORN PARTY

1. Use popcorn markers and a die.
2. Each player places a marker on the "Popcorn Popper" space.
3. The first player throws the die and moves the correct number of spaces.
4. The player must name the picture in the space and make a sentence using that word before the other players can count to 10.
5. If the player names the picture and makes the sentence, he may move ahead one space. If not, the player moves back two spaces.
6. The first player to reach the "Popcorn Party" wins!

Kernels

Sugar and spice

cloves

BALLOONS

Party HATS

Popcorn Balls

Popcorn Party

Ear

Shucks

Butter

Snack

Salt

Popcorn Popper

© 1989 by Incentive Publications, Inc., Nashville, TN.

HALLOWEEN

Major Objective:
Children will develop appreciation for the folklore associated with Halloween and will become familiar with the symbols, characters, colors and literature related to this fun holiday.

15 Terrific Tips For The Happiest Halloween Party Ever!

The teacher will be as happy as the children with these quick-and-easy, no-fail, no-fuss, no-mess, no-stress, no-strain suggestions!

1. Place a white paper plate, cup and napkin in a medium size brown paper bag for each child. For party entertainment, have the children use orange and black crayons to decorate their bags (for use as place mats), cups, napkins and plates. (Have the children color on the back sides of plates and the outsides of cups so that crayon wax will not be eaten.)

2. Let the children tear white paper to make one-of-a-kind ghosts. String the ghosts from every window and door to give the room a festive look. Read *Gus and the Baby Ghost* (see page 77).

3. Let the children play "October-O" (same rules as BINGO). Each child will need a calendar and calendar art squares (pages 12 & 13). Give instructions such as: "Under Monday, paste a pumpkin; under Wednesday, paste an owl," etc. Award the winner with a special party favor or privilege!

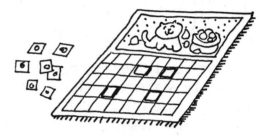

4. Have each child wrap and secure a tissue around a lollipop to make an extraordinary ghost! Eyes, a nose and a mouth can be added with a crayon.

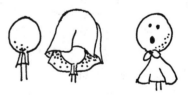

5. Serve witches' brew directly from the orange juice bottle. Simply drop a little orange food coloring or red maraschino cherry juice into the bottle!

6. Buy enough big round cookies for the class. Provide bowls of orange frosting and let the children turn cookies into jack-o'-lanterns (a toothpick makes a good "drawing" tool).

7. *Orange Frosting Recipe:* Mix confectioner's sugar with just enough milk to give it a spreading consistency. Add orange food coloring and a few drops of orange extract. Stir until smooth and spread on the cookies.

8. Have each child color a pumpkin pattern (page 40) to make a personality jack-o'-lantern (be sure the children write their names on the backs of their pumpkins). Line up the jack-o'-lanterns and let the children vote on the best personality.

9. Present the "Top Pumpkin" award (page 15) to the winner of the personality jack-o'-lantern contest!

10. Ask the children to act out the "moods" of their jack-o'-lanterns. Let each child tell what happened to cause the jack-o'-lantern to feel that way.

11. Use the pumpkin pattern (page 40) to make jigsaw puzzles for the party.

12. Enlarge the pumpkin pattern on page 40. Draw facial features on the pumpkin and cut out a mouth. Blindfold the children and play "feed the pumpkin."

13. Let each child contribute one or two sentences to a spooky story that you begin.

14. Provide the children with strips of black and orange construction paper and paste. Have the children make Halloween jewelry to wear during and after the party! (Demonstrate how to split, double, twist, twirl and link strips.)

15. When the party is over, have the children place all of the party debris in their brown paper bags and deposit the bags in the trash as they leave the room! When it's time to go home, you'll be able to go home, too!

HALLOWEEN SAFETY

1. Wear a Halloween costume that will not cause you to trip or fall and a mask that allows you to see clearly.

2. If you are not wearing light-colored clothes, be sure to attach reflecting tape to your costume. Be careful when crossing streets.

3. If an adult is not with you, make sure that an adult knows exactly where you are going, who is going with you, and how long you will be gone.

4. Do not walk in the street.

5. Stay away from houses that are not well lit.

6. Accept treats only from people you know.

7. Do not eat anything from your bag until it has been checked by an adult.

8. Never eat candy or chewing gum that has been unwrapped.

9. If you put a candle inside a jack-o'-lantern, be sure to place the jack-o'-lantern away from walls or other objects that could catch fire.

© 1989 by Incentive Publications, Inc., Nashville, TN.

1989 by Incentive Publications, Inc., Nashville, TN.

HALLOWEEN HOUSE HOW-TO'S

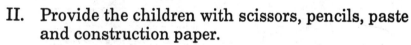

I. Reproduce and distribute the *Halloween House* and *Halloween Creatures* patterns on pages 56 and 57. Provide the children with scissors and crayons.

Ask the children to:

1. Color and cut out the Halloween house.
2. Cut along the dotted lines to make slits in which to insert the Halloween creatures.
3. Fold back the window shutters and the door of the Halloween house.
4. Color and cut out the Halloween creatures.
5. Insert the tabs of the Halloween creatures in the slits in the Halloween house. (Encourage the children to place the Halloween creatures in slits of their choice in order to create their own "scenes.")

II. Provide the children with scissors, pencils, paste and construction paper.

Instruct the children to:

1. Fold the construction paper vertically to make a booklet.
2. Draw or write a creative story on one side of the booklet about the Halloween house and its special Halloween creatures.
3. Paste the Halloween house with its Halloween creatures on the other side of the folded booklet.
4. Write the title of your story and your name on the outside of the booklet.
5. Take the booklet home to share with family members.

© 1989 by Incentive Publications, Inc., Nashville, TN.

HALLOWEEN HOUSE

© 1989 by Incentive Publications, Inc., Nashville, TN.

HALLOWEEN CREATURES

© 1989 by Incentive Publications, Inc., Nashville, TN.

... MORE THINGS TO DO

1. Add tabs to the Halloween creatures to make finger puppets. Make up puppet plays and let groups of children present them to the class.

2. Ask the children to cut free-form construction paper witches, ghosts, goblins, etc. to complete the scene. Use the scene as a background for displaying the children's work.

3. Paste the Halloween house and creatures on trick or treat bags.

4. Enlarge the Halloween house pattern and use it for a bulletin board display.

5. Color and cut out the creatures and use them for figures in a shoe box peep show display.

FLYING BAT

Do not cut out bat.

1. Lay page face down and fold back diagonally along line **A**.

2. Fold point **A** down to meet point **A**.

3. Fold point **B** down to meet point **B**.

4. Fold along line **C** (so that the Bat is showing).

5. Fold wings up along lines **D**.

6. Fold wing tabs up along lines **E**.

© 1989 by Incentive Publications, Inc., Nashville, TN.

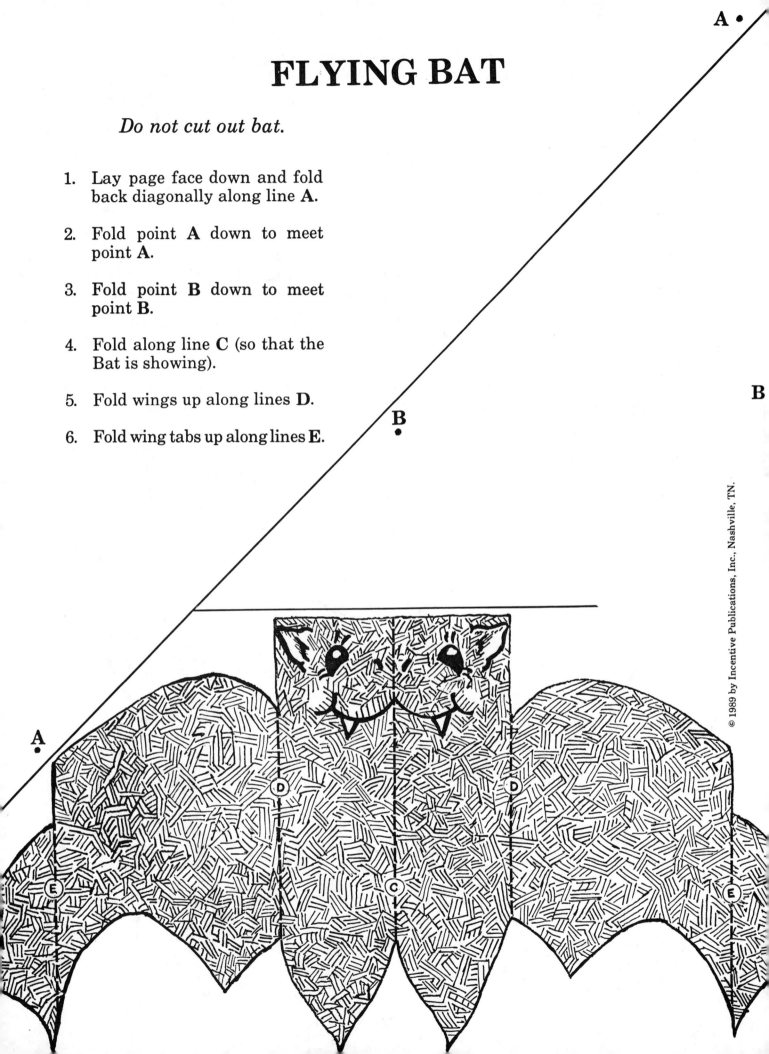

BAT MOBILES

1. Have the students work together in groups of three or four to make bat mobiles.

   a. Tie two twigs together with black yarn to make an X, extending the yarn at the top to make a loop for hanging.

   b. Cut out several bats and color them with crayons or markers. Punch a hole in each bat and suspend the bats from the twigs with different lengths of black yarn. (Note: Coat hangers may be used if twigs are not available.)

2. During the construction of the mobiles, discuss the concept of balance and present examples such as seesaws and pulleys that require equal weight on both sides.

3. When the mobiles are completed, have the students slip plastic knives, small stones or thin pencils into the paper folds to "unbalance" the bats. Discuss the results.

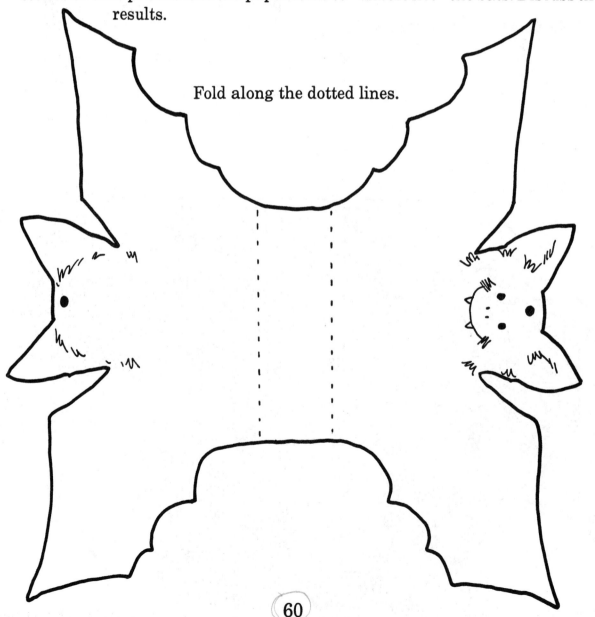

Fold along the dotted lines.

© 1989 by Incentive Publications, Inc., Nashville, TN.

Fold along the dotted lines

© 1989 by Incentive Publications, Inc., Nashville, TN.

BOBBY HAD A
SMALL BLACK CAT

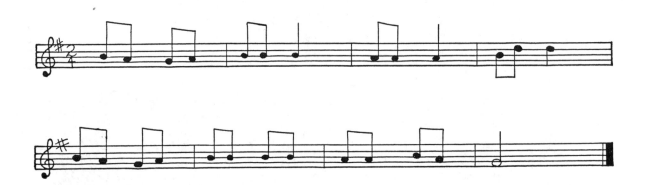

Sung to the tune of *Mary Had A Little Lamb.*

Bobby had a small black cat,
Small black cat, small black cat,
Bobby had a small black cat,
Its coat was black as coal.

It followed him to school one day,
School one day, school one day,
It followed him to school one day,
That was against the rule.

It made the children laugh and play,
Laugh and play, laugh and play,
It make the children laugh and play,
To see a cat at school.

And so the teacher turned it out,
Turned it out, turned it out,
And so the teacher turned it out,
But still it lingered near.

Why does the cat love Bobby so,
Bobby so, Bobby so,
Why does the cat love Bobby so,
The eager children cry.

Why, Bobby loves the cat you know,
Cat you know, cat you know,
Why, Bobby loves the cat you know,
The teacher did reply.

© 1989 by Incentive Publications, Inc., Nashville, TN.

STAND-UP WITCH

Cut out and color the witch.
Paste the witch together at
the dotted line.

Suggested Reading:
Humbug Witch (see page 77).

© 1989 by Incentive Publications, Inc., Nashville, TN.

Name _____

WHICH WITCHES ARE EXACTLY ALIKE?

One little, two little,
Three little witches,
Four little, five little,
Six little witches,
Six litle witches
Flying through the air.
Six little witches
Without a care.

Six little witches all look the same.
But only two little witches are exactly alike.
Look carefully and circle the two little witches that are exactly alike.

Make up a story about the witches.

Visual discrimination: seeing likenesses & differences
© 1989 by Incentive Publications, Inc., Nashville, TN.

© 1989 by Incentive Publications, Inc., Nashville, TN.

Name _____

ON THE RIGHT PATH

Trace a path to help the little ghost get to the party.
Tell his tale.

Visual discrimination & storytelling
© 1989 by Incentive Publications, Inc., Nashville, TN.

© 1989 by Incentive Publications, Inc., Nashville, TN.

Goblin

Gremlin

Suggested Reading: *Dorrie and the Goblin* (see page 77).

© 1989 by Incentive Publications, Inc., Nashville, TN.

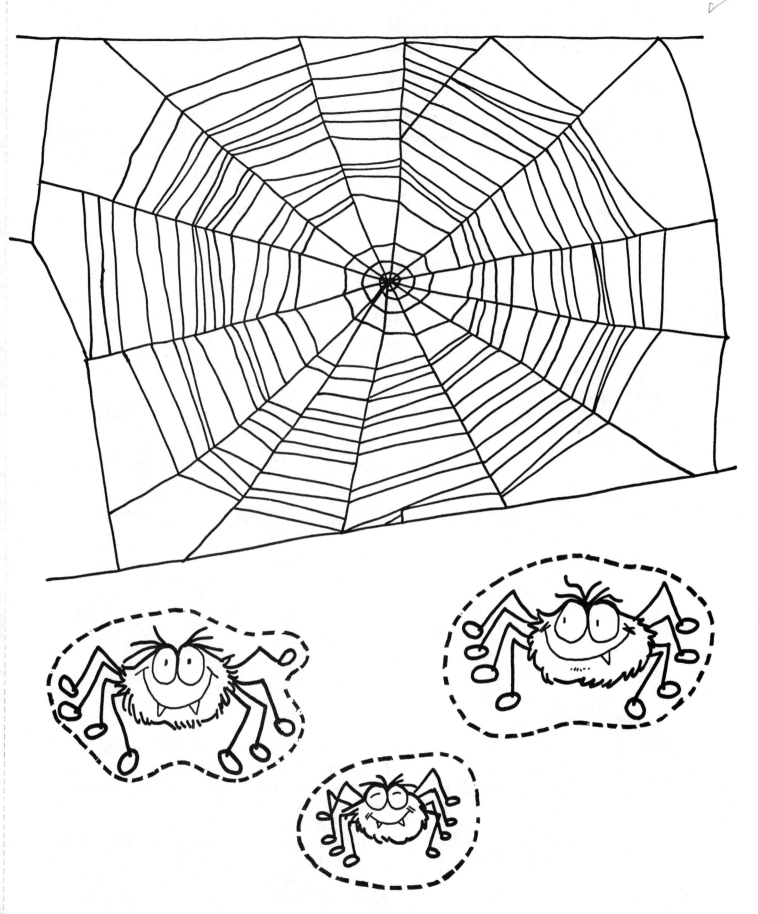

Use the patterns to present a finger play of *The Eensie, Weensie Spider*.

© 1989 by Incentive Publications, Inc., Nashville, TN.

HALLOWEEN PIÑATA

What To Use:

newspaper
1 large & 1 small paper
   sack
rubber bands or string
masking tape
paste

orange construction paper
black construction paper
black tissue paper
candy & treats
scissors

What To Do:

1. Shred newspaper and stuff it into a large paper sack.
2. Fill the sack with candy and treats. Secure the opening with rubber bands or string.

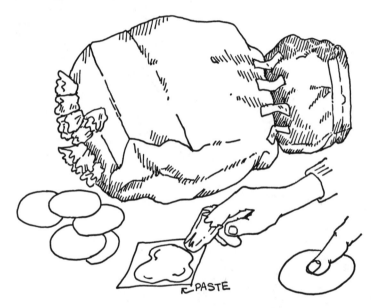

3. Stuff a small paper sack with shredded newspaper and attach the sack to the "body" with masking tape.

4. Have the children cut circles out of black tissue paper. Have each child wrap a tissue circle around his or her index finger, dip the circle in paste, and attach it to the spider to cover the head and body.
5. Cut eyes and a mouth out of orange construction paper and paste them to the head.
6. Cut 8 long strips out of black construction paper. Bend each strip in the middle and paste four strips to each side of the body for legs.

MONSTER MASK

Cut out and color this monster mask to make it scary enough to
frighten even your teacher!
Punch a hole in each side of the mask.
Run yarn or string through the holes.
Tie the mask behind your head.

© 1989 by Incentive Publications, Inc., Nashville, TN.

THE EASIEST MASK EVER

Cut out and color the mask.
Punch a hole in each side of the mask.
Run yarn or string through the holes.
Tie the mask behind your head.

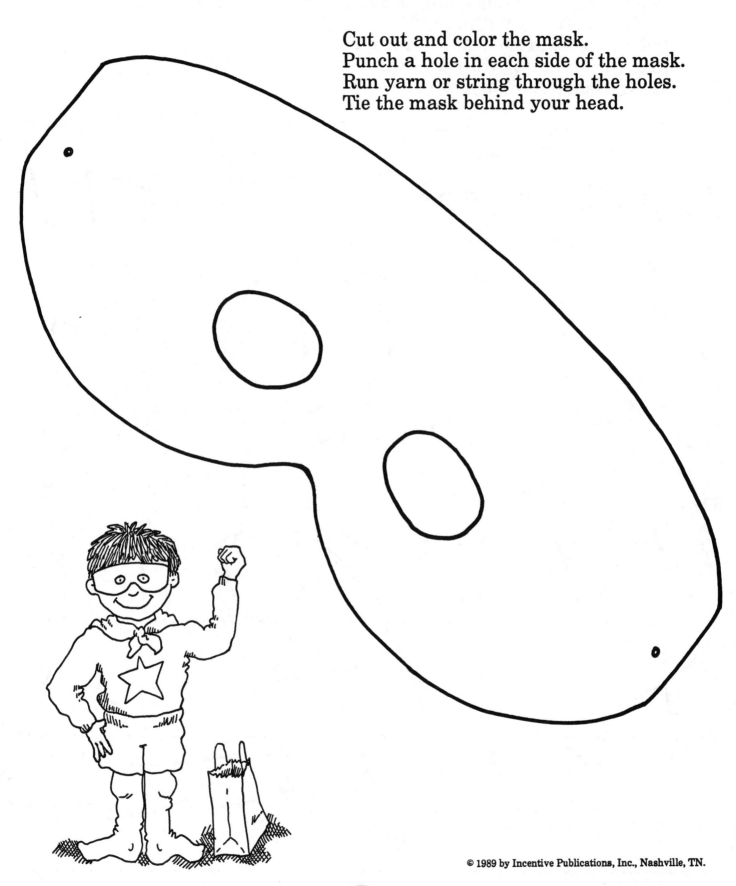

© 1989 by Incentive Publications, Inc., Nashville, TN.

Name _____

DINOSAURS
FOR HALLOWEEN

Halloween is a time when you can be anything you want to be.
These children wanted to be dinosaurs.
Cut and paste the dinosaur names under the correct costumes.
How many other dinosaurs can you name?

Brontosaurus   Stegosaurus   Tyrannosaurus

Recognizing dinosaurs
© 1989 by Incentive Publications, Inc., Nashville, TN.

BRONTOSAURUS COSTUME

© 1989 by Incentive Publications, Inc., Nashville, TN.

STEGOSAURUS
COSTUME

© 1989 by Incentive Publications, Inc., Nashville, TN.

TYRANNOSAURUS COSTUME

© 1989 by Incentive Publications, Inc., Nashville, TN.

BIBLIOGRAPHY

The Aesop for Children. Checkerboard Press.
This full-color edition of the classic Aesop contains 126 of the best-loved fables.

Bumps in the Night. Harry Allard. Doubleday & Company.
Dudley Stork invites his friends to a séance to help him rid his house of things that go bump in the night.

Dinosaur Learning Fun. Imogene Forte. Incentive Publications.
This book contains read-and-color pages, fun activity sheets, and stand-up dinosaur figures to teach young children about 11 dinosaurs.

Dorrie and the Goblin. Patricia Coombs. Lothrop, Lee & Shepard Co.
When a goblin is found hiding in a laundry basket, Dorrie volunteers to goblin-sit so that Old Witch and Cook can prepare for the tea and magic show. After several mishaps, Dorrie saves the day.

A Fairy Tale Treasury. Raymond Briggs. Hamish Hamilton Children's Books, Ltd.
This collection of favorite fairy tales contains something for all children.

The Ghost Said Boo. John McInnes. Garrard.
Claude the ghost tries desperately to scare the animals in the barn. When he finally scares them, he discovers that he would rather be friends.

Gus and the Baby Ghost. Jane Thayer. William Morrow & Co.
This is the story of what happens when Gus the ghost finds a baby ghost on the steps of the historical museum in which he lives.

The Halloween Party. Lonzo Anderson. Charles Scribner's Sons.
This is the tale of Faraday Folsom's adventures as he makes his way to a Halloween party.

The Halloween Pumpkin Smasher. Judith St. George. G.P. Putnam's Sons.
Mary Grace Potts and her imaginary friend Nellie do some investigative snooping to find out who has been smashing all of the pumpkins on Grove Street.

Halloween Surprises. Ann Schweninger. Viking Penguin, Inc.
Buttercup and Button Brown Rabbit make costumes, carve jack-o'-lanterns, and go trick-or-treating with their family. Just when the fun seems to be over, their parents give them one last wonderful surprise.

Heckedy Peg. Audrey Wood. Harcourt Brace Jovanovich.
When seven children named Monday, Tuesday, Wednesday, Thursday, Friday, Saturday and Sunday fall under a witch's spell, only their mother can save them.

Humbug Witch. Lorna Balian. Abingdon Press.
A little witch tries her best to do all of the things witches do, but nothing seems to work. The surprise ending will delight children.

Lizzie the Lost Toys Witch. Mabel Harmer. Macrae Smith Co.
A kangaroo follows Lizzie the Lost Toys Witch home one evening and causes all kinds of mischief.

Mother Goose, The Classic Volland Edition. Eulalie Osgood Grover, ed. Hubbard Press.
This classic edition of "Mother Goose" with its beautiful illustrations will delight children of all ages.

The Mouses' Terrible Halloween. True Kelley & Steven Lindblom. Lothrop, Lee & Shepard.
As the Mouse family gets ready for Halloween, they experience unexpected adventure at every turn.

Old Mother Witch. Carol Carrick. Seabury Press.
When David's friends dare him to ring Mrs. Oliver's bell on Halloween night, David discovers that something really frightening has happened. The story ends on a gentle note of understanding.

Old Witch Rescues Halloween. Wende & Harry Devlin. Parents' Magazine Press.
Old Witch uses her magic to save the town of Oldwick from Mr. Butterbean's attempt to stop Halloween.

Outside Over There. Maurice Sendak. Harper & Row.
After goblins steal the baby from its cradle, Ida sets out with her horn in hand to "catch those goblins with a tune" and save her baby sister.

The Oxford Picture Word Book. Anne Nelson & Sue Hale. Oxford University Press.
This book contains 800 words children need when learning to read and write. The main part of the book consists of 550 words in alphabetical order, each accompanied by a phrase and an attractive picture.

Pleasant Fieldmouse's Halloween Party. Jan Wahl. G.P. Putnam's Sons.
The mysterious capers that precede the Halloween party guarantee a night of surprises for everyone.

Proud Pumpkin. Nora S. Unwin. E.P. Dutton & Co.
A big, proud orange pumpkin learns that it's nice to be useful after all.

Pumpkin Pumpkin. Jeanne Titherington. Greenwillow Books.
A little boy plants a pumpkin seed in the spring, watches it grow in the summer, carves it at Halloween, and saves six seeds for planting.

Rapunzel from the Brothers Grimm. Retold by Barbara Rogasky. Holiday House.
This is the classic story of a lovely young girl who is raised by a witch and locked up in a tower until she is finally rescued by a handsome prince.

Seasons. John Burningham. The Bobbs-Merrill Co.
This is a collection of seasonal scenes in extravagant color with simple text.

Sing a Song of Popcorn. Poems selected by Beatrice Schenk de Regniers, Eva Moore, Mary Michaels White, & Jan Carr. Scholastic.
This stunning collection of poetry ranging from ancient to contemporary is illustrated by nine Caldecott Medal-winning artists.

Suzette and Nicholas and the Seasons Clock. Marie-France Mangin. Philomel Books.
This beautifully-illustrated book about the special delights of each season contains directions for making a seasons clock which may be used with the story.

The Thorn Witch. E.J. Taylor. Alfred A. Knopf.
As Violet Pickles and Ruby Buttons make their way to a costume party, they are taken prisoner by the Thorn Witch.

The Three Wishes. Margot Zemach. Farrar, Strauss & Giroux.
In this charming fairy tale, three wishes are "wasted" on a pie!

Thumbeline by Hans Christian Anderson. Newly translated by Richard & Clara Winston. William Morrow & Co.
Tiny Thumbeline experiences many trials as she is subjected to the whims of larger creatures. She finally finds happiness with a tiny prince.

The Witch's Hat. Tony Johnson. G.P. Putnam's Sons.
When a witch's hat falls into a big black pot of magical brew, the mischievous magical pot disguises the hat and plays one trick after another on the witch.

Word Bird's Fall Words. Jane Belk Moncure. The Child's World, Inc.
Little Word Bird builds a house in which to put lots of fall words.

INDEX